THE *Evangelist,*

THE HEART OF A

PASTOR

Trilogy Christian Publishers
A Wholly Owned Subsidiary of Trinity Broadcasting Network
2442 Michelle Drive | Tustin, CA 92780

Manufactured in the United States of America
10 9 8 7 6 5 4 3 2 1
Library of Congress Cataloging-in-Publication Data is available.
ISBN 978-1-64088-024-5
ISBN 978-1-64088-025-2 (ebook)

The Work of an *Evangelist,* The Heart of a Pastor

TYLER JERNIGAN

FOREWORD

I am sure that I am not the only dad that has had the opportunity to write the foreword in his son's first published work. Those who have done so are the only ones who could understand my feelings while penning these words.

From the early days of Tyler's life, I sensed the Lord's hand upon him. He was a normal kid, and yet somehow, I knew there were things that he did and ways in which he acted that were not so normal. Even when he was a young boy, it was music and ministry that made up the bulk of his interests. You would think with having a dad who was a pastor, and with all the time spent in church and around church activities and church people, that he might get tired of that kind of life; but no—not Tyler. When we were not at church, he was having church. When we were not involved in music, he was playing music. When he was not hearing a preacher preach at church, he was listening to preachers preach. It was just obvious that God was preparing Tyler, even from his youngest years, for ministry.

As the years flew by, Tyler's gifts and talents developed more and more. I used to try to help him on the piano with chords that I used and methods I had developed, and he finally told me, "You do it your way, and I will do it my way." I realized that God was teaching him, so he had a much better teacher than I could have ever been. There are some characteristics that he cannot escape that I have contributed to his life and ministry. I am thankful each time I see and hear them.

God supernaturally accelerated ministry opportunities for Tyler at age 15. The exposure he received from a God-appointed revival launched ministry opportunities for him that continue even today. He will share that in more detail in this book. Almost overnight, ministry became full time for him.

I could go on and on, sharing how God has directed and blessed this ministry. A lengthier foreword would not be adequate to describe it, because words simply cannot describe it. It is truly amazing what God can do with those who will trust Him.

I believe the following pages will bless you as you read them. This is a testimony of the goodness of the Lord. I am very proud and thankful for Tyler, and even more so for the privilege of being a part of God's plan for his life.

INTRODUCTION

Life is a journey full of ups and downs' hills and valleys. Sinner or saint, life can sometimes be wearying. My journey is no different than yours, but I feel like we can all learn from each other if we are willing. Therefore, this book is a journey through… my journey so far. I am relatively young, but I want to share some of my experiences with you. Maybe they will help somebody. I must admit that while the lessons were being taught, I wasn't always willing to learn. My attitude wasn't always positive.

Granted, there is no eternal impact in my experiences. I am no martyr. I have not suffered for the cause of Christ. Any "suffering" I feel like I have gone through is a skip through the roses compared to others who have literally given their lives for Jesus.

But as an "old soul," I want to write to other "old souls." I want to write to that young man or young woman who feels like they were born in the wrong generation. I want to write to young people who feel called to something greater. You may be in middle school or high school and wonder, "What kind of impact can I have?"

I want to write to those who feel stuck on their journey.

Whoever you are and wherever you are, will you turn the page and walk with me?

CHAPTER 1

I was born to Charles Ray and Sharon Jernigan on April 23, 1993. My parents were told that they couldn't have any more children. The doctors encouraged them to stop trying, because the bad news discouraged them more and more each time. One day, my mom became very ill. After several days of sickness, she determined that she had the flu. However, after she took a pregnancy test behind my dad's back, it turned out that the flu she thought she had was me.

Sampson County is my home. I live in the eastern part of North Carolina in the rural town of Clinton. In case you don't know, it is the hog capital of the world. Imagine how awesome Clinton smells.

When I was growing up, we lived in the sticks of Sampson County. Our nearest neighbors were two miles down the road. My older brother and sister are ten years older. My younger brother is six years younger. I am truly the "monkey in the middle," but middle kids rule!

When I was a kid, I wasn't old enough to keep up with my older siblings, and I didn't want to play with a baby. I wanted to play with all my city friends who lived too far away to congregate at my house, which was surrounded by fields and woods. And on top of the isolation our living situation caused, my dad was a local pastor. I was a preacher's kid.

I attended a Christian Academy in Clinton which eased the pressure for an elementary-aged "PK," but even in a Christian school my peers expected perfection from me.

It wasn't so bad in elementary school, but it really kicked in during the middle school years. I lost my temper one day and the first thing out of my best friend's mouth was, "Your daddy is a preacher!" I carried that stigma throughout my school years.

I come from a line of preachers. My grandad on my mom's side of the family is a retired preacher. My great-uncle on my dad's side of the family is a retired preacher. Everyone I talk to either seems to know my grandad, L.D., or my uncle, Ralph. On both sides of my family, ministry is the norm.

My great-grandad, Lewis Jernigan, was a lay preacher. He never pastored a church, but he was, in every sense of the word, a man of God.

When he was serving as a counselor at Falcon Youth Camp one year, two boys in his cabin ran away and went missing. While the staff, police, and parents were in a panic, my great-grandad was praying. The Lord revealed a certain area to him, he went to that area, and the two boys were there.

While riding his horse and buggy one day, Great-Granddaddy passed by a man with crutches on the side of the road. The man cried out, "Mr. Jernigan! Mr. Jernigan! Please pray for me." My Great-Granddaddy got down beside the man, prayed for him, and got up to get back in the buggy. The man said, "Wait! What do I do with my crutches?" My Great-Granddaddy replied, "Throw them in the ditch! Either you believe, or you don't." He was known as a man of prayer.

I do not take my heritage for granted from either side of the family.

I feel like the psalmist when he said, "The lines are fallen unto me in pleasant places; yea, I have a goodly heritage." (Psalm 16:6 King James Version).

I believe I have many of the blessings I enjoy today because of those who have gone before me.

It would do us good to realize that we are standing on the

shoulders of past generations.

Are we providing strong shoulders for the next generation?

Life was good. Looking back, I can see that I didn't realize how good I really had it. My parents modeled love for Christ and for each other to us.

As I stated earlier, my older brother Jack and my sister Crystal were ten years older than me. Jack drove me around in his Jeep, and Crystal drove me around in her Mustang. They took me to the movies and to different places around town, but I was still very young when they moved away from home.

My "baby" brother and I grew up riding four-wheelers in the fields around our house and playing Nintendo 64 and Game Cube.

In addition to our four-wheelers, Jacob and I had a side-by-side. On summer afternoons, that's all we did. I can't tell you how many times we rode the fields around our house, listening to music and enjoying God's creation. Except one day. One day, Jacob killed God's creation: a blue bird. Since you're not supposed to kill blue birds, we had to dispose of the body before our parents found out about it.

He and I are close friends to this day.

My grandparents lived just a few miles up the road, so most Saturday nights were spent with them, watching Nickelodeon and eating "Ma's" food.

When I was 7 years old, however, my life quickly changed.

I started to become insatiably thirsty. I had to be excused from class several times a day to go to the water fountain. I slept with water bottles beside my bed. No matter how much water I drank, I couldn't be satisfied. My excessive thirst led to bed-wetting, which was extremely embarrassing. My parents decided it was time for a doctor visit.

I can still remember sitting in the exam room at Clinton Medical Clinic, the doctor coming in with his clipboard and with his glasses slid half-way down his nose. He looked at my parents and very solemnly said, "Mr. and Mrs. Jernigan, you need to go home, pack your bags, and take Tyler to UNC Chapel Hill Hospital. I've already called and reserved a bed. Tyler has Type I Diabetes."

My mom answered, "Okay, that's fine. Are you going to prescribe an antibiotic? When will he be better?" Doctor Newton replied, "Mrs. Jernigan, I don't think you understand."

When he had thoroughly explained what was going on, he grabbed our hands and prayed. I can remember, as a 7-year-old, seeing my mom and dad cry. It was at this point that I panicked. I ran out into the hallway and grabbed the nurse and cried.

My life was changing. I just didn't understand it all yet.

As we started the hour-and-a-half trip from the quaint town of Clinton to the booming town of Chapel Hill, the journey was just getting started.

CHAPTER 2

It took a little over a week, but we finally came home from UNC Chapel Hill Hospital. I was starting to grow accustomed to the insulin shots I had to take after every meal and before bedtime. The finger pricks weren't hurting anymore. It was a big adjustment, especially when I couldn't eat Fudge Rounds and drink Coca-Cola any time I wanted to. But life went on.

That insatiable thirst went away, but there was another insatiable thirst that I had obtained.

I became obsessed with preaching. I can't tell you how many boxes of cassette tapes I had (and still have) of my dad preaching. When he would preach revivals, the first question I would ask the preacher was, "Do y'all record your services?" Most kids my age were playing with Beyblades and Tech Dudes. I carried cassettes and a small tape recorder around. I fell asleep every night listening to preachers preach. My parents said it was a phase that I would grow out of. But the more tapes I accumulated, the more I wanted to hear.

When I was 10 years old, I asked my school's principal if I could preach in one of our Chapel services. He quickly obliged, and before I knew it, it was Wednesday morning and I was on the Chapel schedule. While my parents sat on the front row and grinned like a sack full of possum heads, I delivered a five-minute message entitled, "Watch What You Say." I brought my tube of toothpaste and demonstrated how it's easy to squeeze it out, but it's not so easy to put it back in.

My dad gave me the opportunity to preach in a Sunday night youth service. The church was packed. I was nervous.

But I preached my five-minute message, "Watch What You Say," with a brand-new tube of toothpaste.

I was only 10 years old. Can a 10-year-old really feel called by God to preach? I think so.

Paul told Timothy, "Let no man despise thy youth; but be thou an example of the believers, in word, in conversation, in charity, in spirit, in faith, in purity." (I Timothy 4:12 KJV).

If you're a young person reading this and you're asking, "Can I really be an example? I don't have that much experience. I'm just a kid,"

remember that David was a kid when he slung a stone with perfect accuracy into the forehead of the giant, Goliath.

Shadrach, Meshach, and Abednego were kids when they made a stand for God, even if it almost turned them into barbeque.

I like what the Bible says about Daniel. He was a young man. Along with his three friends Hananiah, Mishael, and Azariah (names later changed to Shadrach, Meshach, and Abednego), Daniel received a prominent position in the land of Babylon. Daniel 1:4 calls them "children in whom was no blemish."

They were "goody-goody" kids.

"But Daniel purposed in his heart that he would not defile himself with the portion of the king's meat, nor with the wine which he drank." (Daniel 1:8 KJV).

The king laid out an extensive menu for Daniel and his three buddies. It was a high honor to partake of the king's meat and the king's wine. However, Daniel knew that Babylon was not his homeland. He was a stranger there. Therefore, he purposed in his heart BEFORE the meat or the wine was ever placed before him that he would not defile himself. This was not a middle-aged adult making this decision. This was a kid!

Which proves a very valid point: you're never too young to serve God or take a stand for Him.

Don't ever feel like you have to wait until you're a little older before you really get serious about the call of God on your life. Tomorrow is not promised.

God has blessed many young people with an unusual gift of wisdom beyond their years. While wisdom certainly comes with age, God endows it upon the young as well.

II Chronicles 34:1 talks about a king named Josiah. Guess how old he was--8 years old. Was he even tall enough to reach the throne? What about important decisions including finances and hierarchy stuff? Imagine an 8-year-old conducting a staff meeting.

What made the difference? He had a call from God.

Now, every 8-year-old isn't called to be king over a land.

David was anointed to be king when he was just a young 'un watching Daddy's sheep on the backside of the desert. However, he didn't become king until later in life. Did you know that it is possible to receive the call before you walk in the vocation of that call?

It's important not to get behind the Lord, but it's important not to get ahead of Him, either. You'll forfeit your example and influence.

From the age of 10 to the age of 12, I preached youth services here and there.

A prominent pastor in our community, Pastor Lynn Blackburn, even opened his pulpit to me on many Sunday nights. As a kid, I sort of idolized Pastor Lynn. One year for my birthday, my gift from my parents was to spend a day on the golf course with Pastor Lynn, and you couldn't have given me anything that meant more to me than that.

It turned out that this insatiable thirst for God's Word was not "just a phase," as my parents had earlier suggested. This was a call from God on a pale, often sickly kid with buck teeth and a lazy eye.

Maybe you feel unqualified. Maybe you feel like you just don't have it in you. That's what makes you qualified. We've all heard that saying, "God doesn't call the qualified. God qualifies the called."

If God has called you, He will anoint you for the task. Just remember that He receives the glory. If not, we're asking for trouble.

CHAPTER 3

Every time I got an opportunity to preach, it was like Christmas to me. I remember trying to fall asleep on Saturday nights before Sunday morning services. I was literally like a kid on Christmas Eve. I would run over my sermon in my mind. I slept with my Bible and my sermon notes. The opportunity couldn't get here fast enough! I usually spoke for about 15 minutes, but that 15 minutes meant the world to me.

It's kind of amusing to think back to when I was a 13-year-old preacher. I literally had a mullet. When I say "mullet," I mean Billy Ray Cyrus style. I had circular wire glasses and I walked around with Altoids (the tangerine flavor) in my mouth... all the time. I also wore way too much cologne.

I have never been tall, and I was extremely skinny. Therefore, sports were never a possibility for me. I tried out for the basketball team at our school, but I wasn't picked because of my stature.

Music was my thing. I couldn't play sports, but I knew my way around a set of drums and a keyboard. When I wasn't playing or listening to music, I was reading.

I was an awkward 13-year-old. I was shy and timid when I was around people, but on MySpace I was a social butterfly.

I can remember coming home from school, doing my homework, eating supper, and barricading myself in my bedroom. I would turn on preaching cassettes and play The Sims on my desktop until sometime after midnight.

Let me cut to the chase and tell you that I was the biggest nerd you have ever met.

On top of being a nerd, I was a preacher. A 13-year old preacher. A preacher in 8th grade struggling in Math and Geography classes.

It was unique being such a young preacher.

I would watch the preachers on TV and see them sweat profusely and sling their jackets off in the middle of their sermon. One day at school, a group of my friends asked me how a previous speaking engagement had gone. I said, "It was great! I had sweat dripping from my shirt afterwards."

Okay, I was a preacher AND a liar. Not one drop of sweat had fallen from my forehead. I was a good exaggerator!

Thinking about this period of my life makes me cringe.

However, in the midst of my awkwardness, God was about to sovereignly work on my behalf.

In 2007, my dad was preaching in a community revival with several churches and pastors involved. Of course, I went every night.

On the final night of this community revival, my dad introduced me to Dr. Reynolds Smith. At the time, Dr. Smith was a director in the denomination that my dad was ordained through.

Dr. Smith talked to me like all older preachers talk to young wannabe preachers. He had a deep, intimidating preacher's voice. He told me he would mention my name to churches that were between pastors or looking for youth speakers.

I didn't think he would, but he really did it! I mean, he was a conference "head."

He had more on his plate to worry about than a 13-year-old wannabe, right? But the calls started coming in.

Let me stop right here and say this: thank God for older preachers who pour into the lives of young preachers.

How many voices have been silenced because someone wouldn't give them a chance?

God is a generational God. He is not just the God of Abraham. He is the God of Isaac and Jacob too.

I want to thank every mature Christian who has ever taken time with those less spiritual or less experienced than they are.

There will be no legacy if fathers don't pour into sons and mothers don't pour into daughters.

Dr. Reynolds Smith helped me pursue my ministerial license at the age of 15 and continued to spread my name throughout the conference. He has gone home to be with the Lord now, but his influence in my life and ministry is felt to this day.

Thank you, Dr. Smith, for believing in a young wannabe preacher.

I would usually preach in churches that didn't have pastors. Sometimes there were 15 people in the crowd. Other times there were over 100. It didn't really matter to me. I was getting more and more opportunities to preach. I thought I had hit the big time, but it was all training ground.

Keep in mind that during this time, I was 13, 14, or 15 years old. I couldn't even drive, but I was preaching at least three times a month.

During this time, I depended on my mom and dad to drive me to all my speaking engagements.

On Sunday mornings, it was usually Mom and me. On Sunday nights, both Mom and Dad, my brother, my grandparents, and whatever girl had my interest would pile into a vehicle and go together.

There was one sermon I preached everywhere I went entitled, "Give Me This Mountain." I could preach it to you right now without notes. The last time I saw those notes, I had preached it at least 15 times.

When the same people started showing up at different churches, I had to start preparing more sermons.

A connection Dr. Smith made put me in Goldsboro, North Carolina, for a single-night youth event that turned into 13 weeks of revival. I'll talk about that in the next chapter, but I have a couple more comments about my awkward stages before we move on.

I was wrapped up in preaching and ministry, but I was still 13 years old. I had friends who didn't have ministry on their minds.

They knew I was a preacher, but they knew I was a compromiser, too. I often engaged in conversations I had no business engaging in and laughed at jokes I probably shouldn't have laughed at. Even at that tender age, I can remember feeling convicted.

I had a couple of girlfriends. I was 13. Of course I had my eyes on the ladies. Most of them broke my heart, but any "dates" we ever went on were to church services.

Hey, young person: be young. Seize the moment and make it count. You can enjoy your pre-teen years and not compromise. Don't try to grow up too quickly. Enjoy that time.

I know you feel like you'll never reach adulthood, but when you finally get here, you'll be thankful for those awkward years.

Now, about that 13-week revival...

Chapter 4

By 2008 I had "made my rounds" in the local churches. As a 15-year-old, I was establishing a name for myself. By this time, the mullet was gone (thanks to the pleading of my friends). I had my permit, but I didn't like to drive. I usually just rode with guys at school who were a year older than me. That was cool, you know? The Christian academy I attended was a small school; everybody there was like family. It was during these years that I began to cultivate friendships that meant the world to me.

In the 2008-2009 school year I moved up to a different class. Things were different. There was a cool kid in our class named Jacob. I was intimidated by him. I was accustomed to being as cool as I possibly could be (as a nerd) and being the center of attention. But Jacob was established in this new class. I wasn't.

I'm going to have to be honest and say that although everybody else was taken away by him, I didn't like him. But strangely enough, Jacob became one of my best friends in 10th grade. Our friendship really kicked off at the North Carolina State Fair. We found out that we shared a similar music taste, that he was a Christian, that I coveted his shoes and crazy outfits, and that we both liked exploring old, abandoned places. Okay, they were "haunted" places, but that was a bad word at the Christian academy.

Jacob worked as a pizza delivery guy. On some Saturday nights he would pull up in my parents' driveway at 11:30 p.m. We would get online, type in "haunted..." I mean, "abandoned places in North Carolina," and by midnight we were on the road.

Some mornings we didn't get back until 4 or 5 a.m. I would have to preach in a few hours. He would go with me to some of my services. Others, he just left me hanging by myself.

If we ever got hungry, we would randomly drive 45 minutes to the nearest Krispy Kreme and eat two dozen doughnuts together. If we could get back all the money we spent on gasoline and doughnuts, we would probably be rich today.

But I'm not interested in getting any of that money back. The memories we made during that time will last a lifetime.

In January 2016 I received an unexpected phone call that my ghost-hunting, doughnut-eating friend had been in a car wreck and was killed instantly. Although Jacob was a big part of my life in 2008, our lives took us in different directions after graduation. I remember seeing him in town here and there.

But when he passed away, he and I were not even remotely close.

This is a plea to everyone reading this book: do not take the people in your life for granted. If their name comes up on your phone, answer it. Don't say, "I'll call them back later."

You're not too busy to love the people around you if you'll just make time for them.

January 3, 2009 is a date that is etched on my heart. It was a Saturday. There wasn't anything special about it. I was preaching the next day. At this time, my home church was in the process of building a new sanctuary. We held two Sunday morning services to accommodate the crowd. I was preaching in both services on January 4, plus a Sunday night youth service at a rather large church in Goldsboro.

I had a case of the regular Saturday night excitement. I remember watching television with my brother Jacob and going to bed. To go to sleep, I would put my headphones in and listen to music randomly shuffled on my Zune player. I turned the lights out, turned the Zune on, and lay down on my pillow to try to sleep before the eventful Sunday coming up.

Suddenly, the whole atmosphere of my room changed. It was so noticeable that I sat up in my bed. It wasn't a bad change, but it was unusual.

I felt a sudden urge to pray. Have you ever felt that? Have you ever just been going about your normal business and suddenly feel like you need to pray?

I was so stirred (by what I know was the Holy Spirit), I threw the sheets off me, got on the floor beside my bed, and said, "Lord, I don't know what is going on..." and after that, all I remember is bawling like a baby. I'm not talking about crocodile tears. I felt it in the pit of my stomach. Everything in me was responding to His presence in my bedroom. I still had my headphones in, and I remember the song that was playing. It was "Unfailing Love" by Chris Tomlin. This went on for about half an hour, and when I got off the floor and got back in bed, something had changed. Everything Tyler Jernigan had been remained on the floor that night, because I literally gave Him EVERYTHING.

Even while I am describing this to you, I can well remember the peace and joy that flooded my bedroom that night. You don't have to be at church to commune with God.

That was truly a "Bethel moment" for me.

When I say, "Bethel moment," I am referring to the Jacob of the Old Testament. He met God at a place called Bethel. In Genesis 35, the Bible lets us know that he returned to Bethel where God had appeared to him and built an altar. It became a sacred spot for him.

The next morning, I woke up early and preached both

services at my home church.

On the way home from church, my dad commented on the fact that I had never preached like that before.

To have a man who can deliver a sermon like my dad comment on my sermon delivery was a BIG DEAL!

After lunch and a Sunday afternoon nap, it was time to go to Goldsboro. This time, it was just Dad and me. Mom had a prior engagement and my brother didn't want to go to church, so he stayed with my grandparents.

My dad and I made the 45-minute trip to Bethel Church in Goldsboro. It was kind of ironic that "Bethel" was the name of this church.

At the door, I met Pastor Steve Holder. He and my dad were friends from Bible college days. I vividly remember standing in the foyer of the church and hearing Pastor Steve tell us about the 21-day fast the church had just started. After we talked for a while, it was time for the service to begin.

The music was out of this world. I was accustomed to preaching in traditional churches that had a piano player and an occasional bass guitar player. This church had a whole band and a praise team. After the music and preliminaries, it was time for me to preach... and I was ready.

I preached a message I had preached several times before in other churches. The church was very receptive to the message. I gave the altar call and watched teenagers pile onto the altar.

I wasn't really versed in or comfortable with praying with people at the altar at this point in my ministry, so my dad and Pastor Steve assisted me, along with other leaders in the church.

At the end of the night, 15 people had made a profession of faith.

Pastor Steve called my dad and me to the side while people were still praying around the altar. He asked, "What are you doing tomorrow night?" Confused, I said, "Nothing." He said, "Would you be willing to come back and preach again tomorrow night? If it's okay with your parents, I feel like we need you to come back."

My dad obliged, and it was announced that we would go back Monday night to do it all over again.

I couldn't let everybody see my excitement. I was a preacher. I had to be dignified. But when I got in the car, I was like a kid at a carnival! I called everybody I could think of and said, "We have started a revival in Goldsboro!"

It was probably annoying to them, but my excitement was over the top.

We went back Monday night, and there were more people in attendance than there were Sunday night. I preached one of the few sermon outlines I had prepared.

The altar was flooded. More professions of faith were made.

We went back Tuesday night... Wednesday night... Thursday night. By Friday night, there were hundreds of people in the sanctuary. Responses to the altar calls were getting bigger and bigger.

On Saturday night, we made the decision to enter the second week of revival... and it was just getting started.

CHAPTER 5

The second week of the Bethel Church revival in Goldsboro brought a challenge to me. The revival started on January 4,which was the close of our Christmas break from school. Because I was so tired the next day, my parents allowed me to stay home from school.

Even though the revival was going on that first week, I had no problem because I was simply preaching outlines I had previously prepared and had preached at other churches.

But now the second week was here. I was excited, but I was out of outlines. Though I had preached maybe two or three revivals here and there, I had not preached enough meetings to have a wealth of sermons. So here was my challenge.

School started at 8:15 a.m. School released at 3 p.m. My mom, my brother, and I got home from school at 4 p.m. We had to leave to go to revival by 5:30 p.m. (or 5 p.m. if we wanted to stop and eat somewhere). I had no time to prepare sermons except during breaks at school and on the way to church. My dad let me borrow some of his outlines. My high school teacher worked with me and allowed me breaks when I normally wouldn't have had them. But keep in mind that we were taking this revival "night by night." I didn't know from one day to the next if I would be preaching or not. However, at the close of the second week, we entered the third week.

The momentum was building every night. People were calling from long distances and asking for reserved seating. There was an overflow room set up. Services were being live streamed. But volunteers were getting burned out.

After the third week, we took a break on Monday and Tuesday nights and picked back up on Wednesday nights.

When we thought the revival was starting to die down, we had testimonies such as the following.

One night during praise and worship, Pastor Steve approached the stage with a middle-aged lady. He handed her the mic, and she said, "I was driving by this church and something told me to turn around. I don't go to church. I don't know why I pulled in. But when I came in, I knew I wanted to be saved. I have a court appearance tomorrow morning to gain custody of my children. Will y'all pray for me?"

I thought the roof was going to come off the building. I have never seen people rejoice, hug, cry and laugh like I did that night. It happened more than once. People would drive by, turn around, walk in, and ask to be saved.

We had to borrow the parking lots of businesses around the church because there was no more room to park cars. Nightclubs surrounding the church went out of business. It was just a great, great time.

However, as weeks turned into months, I came down with a terrible cough. I found it hard to preach without going into coughing spells. My parents and I figured it was just a passing cold. One night after preaching, I started aching all over. I felt like I had a fever. It felt like the flu.

I woke up the next morning and felt better. I got ready to go to school. When I got to school, I got a pounding headache and terrible nausea. I told my teacher about it and he gathered some staff members around me and prayed. He told me to go lie down in the sanctuary until I felt better.

I remember lying on the front row of Spirit of Life Church. The sanctuary there held close to 500, so it was a large building. The lights were off. I was wrapped up in a blanket, shivering from cold and nausea. My mom sat on the pew beside me. She kept a watch on my blood sugar for me. I didn't feel like I could lift my head.

After an hour of lying there, I became very ill. My mom called my dad to come from work and take me to UNC Chapel Hill Hospital.

I remember lying there, feeling like my heart was going to beat out of my chest. All of a sudden, I heard someone crying a pew behind me. It was my friend Michael. It was break time for our class, and instead of eating with the rest of the students, he came to the sanctuary to pray for me.

My dad showed up, carried me in his arms like a baby, and put me in the backseat of his car.

I can remember feeling the car start to drive down the road. I felt so sick. My head was pounding. My heart was racing. I heard my dad on his cell phone saying, "Pastor Steve, this is Charles Ray." He told Pastor Steve I probably would not be able to preach that night. I remember my stomach falling to my feet. However, Pastor Steve didn't cancel the revival or schedule another speaker. He prayed with my dad on the phone, asked my dad to be available to preach if I couldn't, and said, "Charles Ray, I believe there is going to be a turnaround."

That's the last thing I remember hearing before I finally drifted off to sleep. I woke up 45 minutes later, sat up, and said, "I'm hungry. I want a graham cracker."

Why in the world I wanted a graham cracker, I don't know. I don't even like graham crackers. And I knew I wasn't pregnant! Within 45 minutes, I had regained my appetite and felt normal again. I felt better than I had felt the whole day.

I told my dad to turn around; I didn't need to go to the hospital. There was a literal "turnaround" that took place that day.

Now I'll let you be the judge of whether it was a miracle or not. Some say it was because I took a nap. Others say it was mere coincidence. But regardless of what you think, I preached that night and the revival continued.

I met countless people in the Bethel revival. Some of them I still have contact with.

One of them was a dear lady whom I affectionally called "Grandma," and to this day, she is still like a grandmother to me. She bought our ministry a camera, a tripod, and blank DVDs so that she could have copies of every service she wasn't able to attend! She paid my way to San Antonio one year to attend a pastor's conference. Like a true grandmother, she has spoiled me.

Some I met in that revival I have never heard from again. Still others I pastor to this day.

I don't think I fully realized what was really happening during those 13 weeks.

At the time of this writing, in my personal ministry I have never experienced anything else quite like that. It was a sovereign movement of the Spirit of God for that season of time. Sure, I have experienced tremendous revivals in different areas, but Bethel was unlike anything I have ever witnessed. It served as a launching pad for my ministry.

Though I had preached in church services leading up to January 4, 2009, that is when I officially entered full-time ministry, and I haven't left it yet.

You may not experience a 13-week revival just like that, but the call of God on your life is no less important than His call on mine. I am convinced that everybody has a "Bethel moment." No, I'm not talking about Bethel Church, although I love Pastor Steve and the people there, and the night before I met them all is one of my personal "Bethel moments." I'm referring to the Old Testament Bethel. Every person reading this book has had or will have a moment in life that they will be able to point back to and say, "God met me there. God prepared me there." When life gets tough and you're not sure why you keep doing what you're doing, you can go back and be refreshed just like Jacob was.

I didn't know it yet, but being "refreshed" is essential in ministry.

Every church is different, and every experience will vary.

Buckle your seat belt. The journey is about to get interesting.

CHAPTER 6

The Bethel revival lasted from January to March of 2009.
I met so many people and forged so many relationships. On
the last night, I cried. Not because I felt the presence of the
Lord, but because I didn't want the revival to end! Bethel had
become a part of my life, and I selfishly didn't want to see
it end. But what felt like the end was really the beginning.
Bethel Church became the church home of most of those
who were saved during that revival and is a flourishing body
of believers to this day.

It was a new beginning for Bethel Church, but it was also
a new beginning for the evangelistic part of my ministry.

The very next week, I had my first speaking engagement.
This time it wasn't just a Sunday morning or Sunday night
service. It was a week-end revival beginning on Wednesday
and going through Saturday.

My first revival outside of Bethel Church was at a church
in a community named PinHook. Clinton is New York City
compared to PinHook. (Sorry, PinHookers... or PinHook-
ies... yeah, that sounds better.)

We outgrew the sanctuary on the first night, and the last
few nights were held in the Family Life Center to accommodate the crowds.

It wasn't because I was a dynamic speaker. It was because
I was 15 years old. Everybody wanted to hear this young
preacher.

You don't see flyers announcing a "43-year-old preacher."
It was my age!

I'm sure if I sat here and thought hard, I could name off

the churches that followed the PinHook revival, but it's really all a blur right now. I can say that I preached in and around Goldsboro, North Carolina, and Jacksonville, North Carolina, the most.

Those were my two "hot spots," and generally every revival I preached in 2009 was packed out.

I got my driver's license in April 2009 and started driving a Saturn Ion. Since there was a curfew of 9 p.m. the first six months of having a driver's license, I still depended on Mom and Dad to drive me to revivals. In case you're not familiar with revivals, most of them do not close out quickly enough to be home at a prompt 9 p.m.

Speaking of having my driver's license, I got my first speeding ticket within a matter of months. I was in Goldsboro where the Bethel revival had taken place. The cop clocked me going 50 in a 35. When he asked for my license and registration, I gave the information to him. While he sat in his car, I grabbed my sermon notebook and opened it on my steering wheel. I figured, "Maybe he'll see this and give me a break," but he didn't. He came back to my window with the ticket.

I had never received a ticket, so I didn't know what a ticket looked like. The cop said, and I quote, "Don't worry about this." He also said a bunch of other stuff about a court date, but all I heard was, "Don't worry about this," so I drove away thankful that I hadn't gotten a ticket… I thought.

When I got home, I took the ticket and shoved it in a drawer in my bedroom. It wasn't long before attorneys started sending me letters in the mail.

My mom called me into the living room and said, "Have you gotten a ticket?" I said, "I got stopped a few weeks ago, but he told me not to worry about it." She said, "Where is the paper he gave you?" I went and retrieved the wadded-up ticket from the back of one of my drawers.

That may be another reason Mom and Dad still drove me around for revival services.

One of my best friends, Aaron, started traveling with us. The official ministry team was me, Mom, Dad, my brother Jacob, and Aaron. Aaron was the audio/visual guy. He recorded our services on the camera Grandma had bought and made DVDs available for purchase immediately following the services.

We started operating somewhat of a product table with CDs, DVDs, T-shirts and music.

We caught some flack for trying to "turn the Father's house into a house of merchandising." Some churches asked that we run the product table from the trunk of our SUV.

We weren't trying to be salesmen. There were expenses in evangelism that a lot of people didn't understand.

But the message was spreading, and the phones were ringing.

Boy, those were some late nights. Aaron and I went to the same school, so our teacher worked well with our schedules.

I can remember traveling to revivals, preaching my guts out, stopping at Burger King for a chicken sandwich and a large iced mocha, falling asleep in the car, sluggishly making it to bed, waking up early, and doing it all over again. Oh, the grease and dried-up pieces of lettuce I would get on my church clothes from Burger King and Bojangles at night. We kept the fast food joints in business. If you had cut me back then, I'm pretty sure I would've bled dirty rice.

We mostly stayed within the eastern part of North Carolina, but in January 2010 we branched out into Chesapeake, Virginia for our first "out of state" revival.

It was somewhat like a vacation. Preaching wasn't "work" for me. I loved it! During the day, my parents, Jacob, Aaron and I would explore Virginia, then we would go to the services at night and hang out in the exercise room at the hotel after services.

I'm not sure how much fun all of that was for my parents, but they were always fun to hang around. Jacob, of course, loved it! He was six years younger than Aaron and me, but he hung right with us (which got annoying at times). Aaron and I were 11th graders living life "on the road."

You'll never know how many times we sang "On the Road Again" when on the way to a new revival somewhere.

I loved the road. I loved driving to the middle of nowhere to preach, going through a drive-thru on the way home, and talking all the way home until an hour and a half felt like five minutes.

I'm not sure if it was the road I loved as much as the people I ran the road with.

In the spring of 2010, Aaron and I had a falling-out over a girl, but we realized we cared about each other more than we did her, so that all straightened out.

Revivals were literally every week. Some weeks we would preach Sunday morning to Wednesday night in one place and go Thursday night through the next Wednesday night in another place.

I'm not old. I understand that. But I don't see how I did it. It had to be by the grace of God that my voice was strong enough to preach back-to-back services like that.

There were times I would get tired and burned out.

I remember one revival where I begged my dad to cancel it. After the Sunday night service, I pouted all the way home. Yes, I was an 11th grader, and I pouted. I said, "Dad! These people don't even want revival. They acted like they hated to be there. Can we please just cancel?" He said, "You made a commitment, and you're going to keep it." I'm not sure that anybody was blessed that week because of the begrudging spirit I had.

If you want to meet colorful characters, get into ministry. I could write a whole book about the many faces, shapes, attitudes and motives of revival goers.

In the summer of 2010, Aaron took another ministry opportunity, and it was me and my family again.

A couple of family friends, Bobby and Anthony, started traveling with me extensively.

In October of 2010, my mom and I headed for Virginia. We went to Norfolk this time. Dad and Jacob stayed at home to be at our home church on Sunday. Bobby and Anthony both had to work. It was Mom and me. (I do love that woman.)

We drove there on Friday. I preached Friday night, Saturday night, and Sunday morning. On Sunday morning after I preached, I felt horrible. It was rainy and windy so I figured, after sweating (I really did sweat now) and going out into the elements, that I was probably coming down with a cold.

When we got home Sunday night, I hopped into my truck (the Saturn Ion was long gone; I had sold it for a Ford F-150) and headed to Goldsboro to visit the girl I was dating at the time.

I wasn't there for five minutes before I ended up on the bathroom floor. Waves of nausea were sweeping over me. I called my dad and begged him to come get me.

You see, Dad had advised me to stay home. He could tell I didn't feel well. But he came, carried me in his arms like a baby, and put me in the backseat of his car. This felt familiar.

When I got home, I went straight to bed. I figured I was probably worn down. I had traveled all weekend. It had been a busy week at school the week before. I probably needed rest.

When I woke up Monday morning, I felt worse. I started feeling so bad, I called my grandparents (who lived right up the road) and begged them to get with my parents to come take me to the doctor.

My dad came home from work and took me to the doctor. Mom rolled me in a wheelchair to the doctor's office. After he checked me out and took bloodwork, he said, "Nothing is wrong with you. You're as healthy as you can be. Your blood sugar is a little higher than usual, but nothing to be alarmed about. I'm going to order you some medicine for nausea, but that's about all I can do."

I lay in the backseat of my parents' car. I remember sitting in the line at Clinton Drug Store. I looked up at the ceiling of the family car and felt so alone. I can't really explain how alone I felt.

At 5:30 p.m. I was back in my bed. I had taken a pill and was staring up at the ceiling in my bedroom now. I could hear my parents, my grandparents, my brother, and a couple of friends in the living room. But I was in my bed… flat on my back… praying not to throw up.

My high school teacher came by, knelt by my bedside, and prayed for me. He cried with me. (Pastor Darian, if you are reading this, you will never know what that meant to me.) After he left and closed the door, the next person to come in was Dad. I said, "Dad, this pill is not working. I need another one."

Against his wishes, he gave me another one. I remember looking up and saying, "God, where are you? And what are you doing? Why do I feel like this?"

I had taken two nausea pills and I was wide awake.

I remember sitting up in my bed, picking up my American Government textbook to study for a test I had missed, and waking up the next day with it stuck to the side of my face.

When I woke up, I called the doctor and he advised me to cancel every revival I had scheduled for the rest of the year.

I was still nauseated, and now I was having to call pastors who had scheduled me months in advance and cancel our revivals "because of my health."

I had been in bed since Sunday night. "This must be a bad virus," I thought.

When I was still no better a few days later, we determined I was just burned out.

Think about it.

From January 2009 to October 2010, I preached almost every week.

It has been said that one 45-minute sermon is equal to 8 hours of work on the body. Plus, I was going to school during the day. Not only that; it was my senior year.

I didn't realize how much I was really carrying on my bony shoulders.

I finally gained enough strength to get back to school and catch up on all the work I had missed. I even felt good enough to go to a Night of Worship with some of my friends. But wouldn't you know it, the next day I was back in bed with the same symptoms.

I don't remember how long it went on, but I literally couldn't do anything but go to school and come home.

Since I had gone from preaching nearly every week to not preaching at all, I became depressed.

I went to the wall where my ministerial license was hanging, handed it to my dad and said, "Dad, I'm not preaching anymore. I'm not physically able to do it. I need to find a job doing something else." I was convinced God was through with me.

Why else would I be in this physical state? Why wouldn't He somehow touch me and make me feel better?

Chapter 7

I got over it. If you were expecting a grand answer from God to the question in the last chapter about Him not touching me, I didn't get that. I just got over it. Sometimes, that's all we really need -- to get over it.

Within a few weeks I was back to normal. I was able to return to the pulpit and the journey of life was starting to be enjoyable again.

In January of 2011 we experienced another revival centered around youth. It wasn't a "youth revival" per se, but the youth were the ones who were responding and getting saved.

We continued another week of the revival, and teenagers I had led to the Lord the previous week were now bringing their friends from school and leading them to the Lord. It was a glorious sight watching teenagers pray with each other and intercede for their lost loved ones.

One teen carried a lot of anger, especially toward his dad. Both he and his dad had wandered away from God, even though they were attending church on a semi-regular basis.

The dad rededicated his life to Christ during the revival and started praying for a restoration of his relationship with his son. But his son would not budge. I talked to the son, but it was like talking to a brick wall.

One night the dad was at the altar praying. I watched the son, heavily under conviction, stomp out of the sanctuary. Within a few minutes he came back into the other side of the sanctuary, came to the altar, and fell on his face. Before I could get to him, all the teens involved in that revival (about 15 or 20 of them) had gathered around and led this guy to the Lord.

As soon as he jumped up, he looked like a different guy. His eyes met the eyes of his dad, and I watched these two embrace; both were new men in Christ.

This is what I was accustomed to, and it felt good to be back in the pulpit.

Senior Year was wrapping up and I couldn't have been any more excited to graduate. My three friends Michael, Dianna, Toni and I graduated from high school and went out to conquer life.

Something happened to me in the summer of 2011, though.

I started listening to preachers on CDs and in person who majored on what I call "outward holiness." Looking back, I realize that some of the stuff they said was just pure mean. But somehow, I was drawn to and intrigued by it. It may or may not have been because of a love interest I had (I had way too many love interests going on), but unfortunately it went deeper than just trying to impress a girl.

Remember when Jesus said, "Out of the abundance of the heart, the mouth speaks"? (Luke 6:45 NRSV). He wasn't lying.

I started preaching an "outward holiness" message that completely contradicted the message of hope that I had preached since the very beginning of my ministry.

Please don't misunderstand me. There are sincere preachers and people in the movement that focuses more on outward appearance, but I took the hope and love of Christ completely out of my sermons. In fact, I felt that if I spoke even briefly on the love or mercy of God, I was watering down the Gospel.

My dad was the first one to mention it to me. I felt like

he was just trying to control me. I said some hurtful things to the man who was not only my mentor, but my dad.

I got worse and worse. I still have CDs of some of those messages, and they make me cringe.

Not only did I put believers under unnecessary condemnation over petty things, I made the Gospel nearly impossible to reach for sinners. I started calling other preachers and churches by name, and even forming complete sermons around the demise of other ministries... as an 18-year-old.

Dad talked to me one morning at home and said, "Son, you don't need to call other ministries by name. With the following you have, some people may enjoy listening to some of those ministers you are calling out." I looked back at him and said, "Dad, the apostle Paul called out names."

Wow. Not one of my brightest moments. And yet my dad graciously bore with me (while Mom sat in the corner and cried).

Mom and Dad knew that I was ruining my reputation as an evangelist.

Churches that were once full were now nearly empty when I would preach there.

Some preachers even called and canceled their services with me when they heard the kind of preaching I was doing.

I justified the cancelations by saying, "They don't want the truth!"

Young ministers, be careful to not let pride creep in. That's what was happening to me. I had preached for two full years, bless God, and it was time for me to set the church straight.

I was a "watchman on the wall." I corrected men who had been in ministry before I was even thought of.

Here is the scary thing: I corrected preachers whom I used to listen to on those cassettes that I loved so much. I was biting the hand of the ones who were feeding me.

You may be reading this, saying, "Someone needs to speak out," but that was not my place. First, I was 18. I had no business trying to be God's agent of correction. Second, I was an evangelist, not a pastor. I had no business going into another man's church and tearing his ministry apart.

Thank you, pastors, who bore with me during this time. I'm sorry for any damage I may have done to your church.

My "setting straight" was not limited to the pulpit. I became hard to get along with in general. I started so many Facebook wars. I severed so many friendships. And I did it all "in the name of Jesus."

If you are a minister and you feel it is somehow your duty to call ministers by name or correct others, please remember that the Gospel is "Good News." We have been endowed with the responsibility of preaching the Gospel, not tearing each other apart.

My brother Jacob (only 12 years old at the time) even started mirroring some of my actions. When I saw a post he had made on social media one day, I knew it was because of my influence.

By the time I realized I was in the wrong, I had done a lot of damage. If I had listened to the advice of my parents and other godly influences in my life, I could have salvaged some of my influence.

We all have said, "If I could go back and change _____, I would."

This is one of those things I wish I could change. I wish I could go back in time, grab the 2011 Tyler by the lapels and say, "Shut up before you really mess up!" But I learned and grew through it. I learned balance. I learned humility. I learned grace.

If you are an evangelist, don't try to be a pastor. Preach the Good News and build hope in people through the Lord Jesus Christ.

CHAPTER 8

Regardless of the dwindling crowds, Anthony and Bobby stuck with me. We endured long nights of travel together. But now, I think because I had become so hard to get along with, I traveled alone for a while. Driving to revivals during this time was so different than it was just two years before.

At first, the car was full: my parents, grandparents, brother, and love interest were with me. It then became my parents, brother, and Aaron. More recently, it had been me, Anthony, and Bobby. Now it was just me, and I didn't enjoy the road alone as much as I enjoyed it with other people.

Jacob always went with me if I had to stay overnight somewhere. Our names are most likely marked in many hotels on a "never allow back in" list.

There were times we would stock up on food and eat it all right there in the hotel room. Bags of trash would lay in the kitchenette area until barbeque stains soaked through the floor. We would gorge ourselves on spicy chicken wings during the day, come back to the room at night (with the air conditioner blaring at 60 degrees), and that's all we could smell. We probably dreamed of dancing chicken wings. We were so unsanitary -- but we cleaned up nicely for church.

Jacob and I always looked forward to those long-distance revivals, though. We have always been close, but we formed a bond during those times that lasts to this very moment. My very best friend (outside of my wife) is my brother, Jacob Jernigan.

For my 21st birthday I wanted to go to Walt Disney World. Somehow we had the funds, and we planned our trip to Disney World within a month and a half.

It was enjoyable. I remembered some of the rides from when I had gone as a kid. But when Jacob and I got home from Disney World, we started missing it.

One night we pulled up YouTube videos of different rides... and that night we developed an unhealthy obsession with Walt Disney World. We started planning another trip, we spent many hours watching YouTube videos of Disney rides, and to this very day it is an obsession he and I both share.

The bond we have was strengthened during those out-of-town revival trips.

After I overcame my "church sheriff" kick (Jacob was by my side the whole time), I accidentally swung the other direction. I dove head first into the fads and fashions I had preached so hard against a few months before. I went from preaching in suits to preaching in jeans and t-shirts. I went from listening to Southern Gospel music to heavy Christian rock-n-roll. I tried to be "hip" while I preached. It's kind of sickening.

I guess in all of it, though, I wanted acceptance. I was in search of identity. I no longer wanted to be identified as a hard-nose "church sheriff" that nobody could get along with. Somehow, I forgot that my identity was not in a certain "style" or "fad." My identity was in the call of God on my life.

Identity had always been a huge issue with me.

After the Bethel revival I was still listening to my cassette tapes, and I had accumulated a big collection of tapes by Rev. David Smith. Incidentally, David is a distant cousin of mine and is a prince of preachers. I wanted to BE David Smith. I tried to talk like him. I tried to annunciate like him. I tried to preach like him.

When he showed up to hear me preach one night, it was like a celebrity had come to hear me.

If it wasn't David I was trying to be like, it was some other preacher.

There is nothing wrong with admiring other preachers and learning from their lives and ministries, but you don't have to try to be like them. It has been said nobody loves a preacher like a preacher, and I believe that. I absolutely admire the lives and ministries of many God has placed in my path.

But be who God has called YOU to be while learning from others.

I hadn't quite learned that. So guess what--when the "cool and hip" fad didn't work for me, I swung back the other direction for a couple of months and became a "church deputy" again. I was so wishy-washy.

At one revival you may have heard one thing. At another revival you may have heard another thing.

I was in desperate need of the stability which is found in identity.

While I was evangelizing, I was taking Bible college classes.

I had also assumed the Minister of Music position at my home church, so I was leading worship there.

During this time I started living in a camper in my parents' backyard, because Mom, Dad and Jacob all had to get up early in the morning. I would usually come home late at night and start rummaging through the cabinets for something to eat. I can't cook to save my life, but I can make a mean bowl of Ramen noodles.

Mom and Dad bought the camper and fixed it up for me in the backyard at my request. They weren't too crazy about the idea.

In September of 2012, after a Wednesday night revival service, my mom texted me to ask me to call her. Her mom, my grandmother, had been admitted to the hospital and was not expected to live through the night.

I didn't have much of a relationship with my maternal grandparents growing up. But our relationship had been restored in 2010. At least twice a week after school, I went over to their house and sat for hours, talking to them about ministry and life in general.

The next morning I woke up early, got dressed, and headed to the hospital where my grandmother and much of my family were.

I had to leave straight from the hospital to go to another revival service, but about 30 minutes before I left I went into my grandma's hospital room with my grandad.

She had a fever, so I took a cup of ice and fed the ice to her. She looked up at me, weak and frail, and said, "Tyler, I'm dying." I said, "Grandma! Don't say that. The doctors say you have a rough case of pneumonia. You'll be back home soon." She just looked away.

We talked, I finally heard her laugh, and when it came time for me to leave she said, "Will you pray for me?"

She, my grandad and I grabbed hands, and we prayed. I said, "I'll be back tomorrow to see you, okay?" I kissed her on her forehead.

I went to the revival that night and preached a message entitled "The Perfect Day." It was all about Heaven and what life will be like there.

On Friday morning, my grandma entered that "perfect day." It crushed my heart when my dad called and told me that she had a massive heart attack and had passed away.

The girl I was dating at the time (wow, I've really said that way too many times in this book) was leaving Saturday for a two-week mission trip. My grandma had just died. A familiar sense of hurt was sweeping over me. My heart felt the same way it had back in October 2010.

That Saturday night, I dropped my girlfriend off at her home and cried all the way back to mine. Not only because I was going to miss her, but because of my grandma.

The hurt in my chest was so great that when I got out of my truck in front of my house, I lay on the cool grass and literally shook in pain. I could take you back to the very spot today.

Like a kid, I lay in my parents' room and held my mom while we both cried.

I went to bed and fell into a deep sleep. I dreamed about Grandma. I dreamed that the mission trip was over… only to be awakened by my brother telling me it was time to get up and get ready for church.

I will never be able to explain the dread I felt getting out of bed.

I was off to start another revival that morning, Grandma's visitation was that afternoon, and I would have to preach again that night.

I made it through Sunday morning. I made it through the visitation. But when I stood to read my scripture on Sunday night, I broke down and could not get myself together. I managed to preach through the tears and the pain I was feeling; Monday morning, I would wake up to preach my grandma's funeral along with my cousin and her pastor.

Any time I talk about my grandma in a sermon , someone inevitably comes up to me and says, "If you think it's rough losing a grandparent, try losing a parent."

I can't even imagine. I don't want to imagine. But this pain I was feeling was real.

However, Grandma used to tell me when I was younger (she knew about my insatiable obsession with preaching), "When you are older and preaching to thousands, I'll be looking over the wall, saying, 'That's my grandson.'"

Though I'm not preaching to thousands, I feel like she probably has kept that promise as surely as she said it.

By 2013 I wasn't a "church deputy" anymore, and I wasn't a "cool dude" anymore. I was just Tyler again. But the revivals just weren't as drawing or powerful.

During this time, a young man who had come to several of my revivals asked if he could start traveling around with me.

I didn't really know him, so I was sort of uncomfortable with the idea at first, but I agreed. This guy traveled to every revival I had.

He was in public school, but he didn't allow the late nights to keep him away from the revivals.

Karson became associated with Tyler Jernigan Ministries. He oversaw my website, product table, and newsletters. He connected with people more quickly than I did at times. I watched a shy, timid teenager develop into a confident man of God.

On one occasion, I had a speaking engagement scheduled in Morehead City, North Carolina. Some of Karson's family had a beach house there. He, Jacob and I had a three-story beach house to ourselves for a weekend.

It was December, so it wasn't beach weather, but there was a hot tub, a TV, and plenty of homemade chocolate chip cookies.

It was great, until I ate raw oysters with a greenish tint to them. Jacob said, "Ty, you don't need to eat those." I said,

"There's nothing wrong with them," and ended up with food poisoning and the flu all at the same time.

You don't want to know how I rang in the New Year. Ringing it in wasn't pleasant, but 2015 was here... and a lot was about to change.

CHAPTER 9

It was 2015. As I overcame my food poisoning and the flu, I started looking ahead to revival services with excitement.

I can't adequately describe my feelings about this , but by now in my ministry I was preaching revivals at the churches of men I had heard preach every night before I went to bed. They were calling me by my first name. It was like... we knew each other. I know that sounds ridiculous to some of you, but it's like life had formed a full circle.

I was praying one day as usual. I kind of had a pattern I followed in my prayer time. As I was praying, these words fell out of my mouth, "Lord, give me a pastor's heart."

I remember stopping and putting my hand over my mouth. I backtracked and said, "Lord, I didn't mean that. I don't know where that came from," but those words became a part of my daily prayer.

You see, in my evangelistic meetings I was known for saying, "I'll never pastor a church! You'll never get me to settle down."

Settle down.

I was a free spirit. You weren't going to settle me down to one church... or to one woman either.

Until I met Carry Britt.

Let me pause our story for a moment and rewind to 2012.

I was preaching a revival in Fuquay-Varina, North Carolina, along with another minister. I preached the first part of the week, and he preached the final part of the week.

On Tuesday night of the revival, he brought a van-load of his church members with him. Among that van-load of church members was a girl who caught my eye during my sermon. She didn't speak to me (other than shaking my hand and telling me the sermon was good), and that was the end of that.

In 2014, this same girl showed up at one of my revivals in Lumberton, North Carolina (her hometown). This time, something was different. When she rounded the corner to go into the sanctuary, Jacob and I were standing at my product table. She never looked my way, but as I watched her walk into the sanctuary I said two words, "Goodness gracious."

I made a point to speak to her before the service. I walked confidently over to the pew where she was, tripped over my own two feet, and caught myself on the pew she was sitting on. She looked up at me like I was the plague.

I said, "Hey! How are you?" She said, "I'm good. How are you?" She stood up for a handshake, but I went in for a hug. I said, "I'm good. How are you?" I realized I had made a complete fool of myself.

We messaged each other on Facebook. We texted a little. She attended all the services that week.

Here is where our stories differ. If you were to ask Carry what happened next, she would say that I started ignoring her and standing her up. I believe we were just unclear about our intentions after that week in August of 2014.

I was invited to her birthday dinner in November. I didn't show up. We stopped talking.

One night I was preaching a revival in Leland, North Carolina, when in the middle of my sermon, I looked across the audience and saw her. At least, I thought it was her.

I still have the CD from that service. You can hear my voice crack, and my stuttering gives away that I had been distracted. Was that really Carry? In Leland? After she had been so upset with me?

It bothered me all the way home that night. I texted her the next morning, and like a real champ said, "You must have a twin because I know you weren't in Leland last night! Lol."

She texted back and said, "It was me. Your sermon was good," and we didn't say much to each other after that.

When she found out that I had food poisoning and the flu (which I talked about in a previous chapter), she texted me and asked if there was anything she could do for me. She was being sweet, even though I had "stood her up" several times. We started talking again.

She texted me one day and said, "I'll be in Clinton next week. I'll be at Bojangles at 12:30 p.m. If you're there, that's great. If not, that's okay, too." I didn't know it, but she had made up her mind that if I didn't show up, she was done trying with me.

I remember that day. I got ready an hour early. I sat and watched the clock. When it came time to leave, I got in my truck and headed to Bojangles. I pulled into the parking lot, and her little black car was nowhere to be found.

I pulled to the other side of the building… no black car.

Instead of waiting, I pulled back out onto the road to head back home. When I got about five minutes away, something told me to turn back around. "No. I have to preach tonight. I'm not going to run my gas out riding around Bojangles," but it was like an invisible hand turned my steering wheel, got off the next exit ramp, and turned back around to Bojangles.

When I pulled into the parking lot this time, her little black car was there.

I walked in, sweaty palms and everything, ordered my food, and sat down at a table across from this mysterious girl… and we sat in Bojangles for four hours talking.

You could've stuck a fork in me... I was done! She had my heart. I was love-struck. To make it even better, she stuck around and went to the revival service that night.

An elderly man came up to us and said, "Are y'all a couple?" I quickly answered, "No sir." He said, "Y'all would make a good one. Just saying," and as a southern elderly man would, he winked at us and walked away.

Most of our dates were to church services.

Interestingly enough, I think Carry asked me to be her boyfriend. I don't think I ever asked her out as was the custom (around here, at least). She would sing at my revivals, and I would preach.

One weekend in mid-February, the subject of marriage came up.

I know, I know. We hadn't dated long at all. I had never really thought about marriage. But here we were. Talking about all our plans.

At the beginning of March, I went to Sessom's Jewelry in Clinton and bought an engagement ring.

I didn't have a proposal plan in mind. I wasn't sure when I was going to propose. But I had the ring when I was ready.

I went out to dinner with Carry's mom and dad, whom I love dearly. I told them how much I thought of their daughter, and how I wanted her to be my wife. They both gave me their blessing, which took a huge burden off of my shoulders. (Parents of girls have never been big fans of mine. There have been a few exceptions, but for the most part the parents have been hard to please.)

On the last Sunday morning of March, I was ready. It was a normal Sunday morning. Carry was going to be visiting my dad's church that day. As I was getting dressed for church, I told my mom, "Today's the day."

Before my dad preached that day, I knelt on one knee (for approximately three seconds) and asked Carry to be my wife. She hesitated, and my heart stopped for a while, but she said "yes."

Wedding plans ensued! We decided we would get married on November 7, 2015.

I was so excited! But Carry was so nervous.

When I would talk about the wedding and marriage, she would get uneasy. I started thinking she might back out, but I stayed optimistic. I also knew that if this Cherokee Indian packed up her tee-pee and went off the grid, this Caucasian Pilgrim was going with her!

While we were wedding planning, I was still revivaling. Revivals picked up in 2015. It was my busiest year since 2011.

I also started looking for a house for us to live in. A lot of big decisions were being made in a matter of months.

The only few weeks I had "off" during the summer months of 2015 were spent in the Sampson County Courthouse… on a jury. I had jury duty, and I hated it.

Something familiar was happening to me that I had let happen to me too many times: I was getting burned out.

This guy who was excited about getting married, loved family time, and loved ministry became a cynical, critical, VERY hard-to-get-along-with crab.

I have talked frequently in this book about the special bond my brother Jacob and I share. During this time, I treated Jacob like a stranger. I acted disgusted when he walked my way. You see, I had a sneaking suspicion that Jacob wanted my woman. I allowed my insecurities to almost ruin our relationship.

Our rooms were adjacent to each other in Mom and Dad's house. But I could go days without speaking to him, even if he was directly in front of my face.

In July, my mood lightened a bit when we were finally able to close on a house. I was 22 years old, and I was a homeowner.

While I was trying to move too quickly, my parents were ever in my ear, softly suggesting; I was ever in their faces, abruptly asking them to back out of my life. I even blew up at my dad one day and said, "I'm not your little kid anymore!"

Carry had a job in Clinton by now. She was living in the house.

Although we are both against cohabitating, we were on the verge of doing it.

Not to mention that temptation was so strong during this time.

One day, my dad came to the house to hang some blinds (I'm serious when I say that I can't do anything but preach). I was in the room he was in, and he confronted me about how bad it looked for my car to be visible in that driveway so late at night. He said, "You know, people are watching you." I blew up.

I told him I didn't care what anybody thought, whether it was somebody else in the family or him. I told him I didn't appreciate him and Mom trying to run my life. After I said many more hurtful things to my dad, I stomped through the house and slammed the door to my home office.

He didn't leave. He stayed another hour and hung all the blinds I had asked him to hang. He came and stood at the office door, said, "I love you, son," and quietly left.

Until we sold that house, I couldn't look at the blinds without feeling a sting in my heart, knowing my dad had taken time out of his schedule to help me and I had talked so ugly to him.

Maybe I should have remembered that sermon I preached as a 10-year-old, "Watch What You Say." It was easy to squeeze those words out of the toothpaste tube, but there was no way to put them back in.

While I know God has forgiven me and my dad has forgiven me for such hurtful words and harmful actions, I regret every word I said to him and the way I treated my family.

One Sunday in July I was traveling down Highway 50, on my way to a revival in Chinquapin, North Carolina. (It is pronounced just as it reads, except don't put too much emphasis on the "qu". Use more of a "k" sound there.)

I reached the end of Highway 50 leading onto Highway 41 and as I sat at that stop sign, I felt so stuck. Not at the stop sign, but in life! I hated my life. As blessed and fortunate as I was, I didn't know how to handle it. I didn't want to preach that night. I wanted to go home, get in bed, and sleep my life away. But it turned out that would be another "Bethel moment" for me.

The summer months finally gave way to my favorite time of year: fall.

This fall, everything was much more special. This fall, I was going to be a married man. Carry and I had brought a baby home: a few-week old Chorkie puppy. Her name was Jazzy and she was (and still is) our pride and joy.

It was during the fall of 2015 that I met one of my "preacher heroes."

For my dad's Pastor Appreciation service in September, I wanted to plan something big. I called one of his favorite preachers, Pastor Larry McDaniel, and asked him if he would be willing to come from Georgia and speak.

Dad had passed all of the McDaniel cassettes that he had gathered in his early ministry down to me.

Talking to this man whom I had heard preach so many times was surreal.

Pastor McDaniel came, and our families were knit together. He and his dear wife, Mrs. Annette, have had us in their home as guests.

Carry and I even stopped off at their church on our way home from our honeymoon. Any time we go to the Sunshine State, we stop in Georgia to see the McDaniels.

The last time Carry and I visited Pastor Larry and Mrs. Annette, we drove with Pastor Larry to downtown Savannah.

Carry makes fun of me, but I was so nervous, I almost pulled out in front of a vehicle and almost threw Pastor McDaniel through the windshield.

That is just another example of God bringing things full circle. Pastor McDaniel is another man whom I had tried to annunciate like and preach like for a while.

And now, I have his personal number in my phone and he and I have texted. That's so crazy!

Anyway, back to our story…

Amid all of this, my temper had not gotten any better. Not only had I treated my parents and my brother so hostilely, now I was turning my anger toward Carry.

The laughs and smiles we were accustomed to had turned to screams and sarcasm… and we hadn't even gotten married.

In October, late one night I told Carry I wasn't sure if I wanted to marry her anymore.

After a heated conversation she took her engagement ring off, laid it in my lap, and walked out the door. I watched her little black car--the same little black car I had looked for so anxiously at Bojangles at the beginning of the year--pull out onto the street and speed off. I didn't know where she was going and frankly, I didn't care.

I cannot convey to you how angry a person I was. I don't know what had made me this way. People whom I cherished and loved were being treated like trash because of my temper.

I called my mom, and when she answered I screamed through tears, "Carry just left."

Jazzy was in her kennel, whining. I think she was sympathizing with me.

My mom and Jacob came and sat with me for a while.

Carry had come back. We all sat in the living room and Carry apologized. I still don't know why she apologized. And I don't know why Mom and Jacob came, especially after I had treated them the way I had.

I told everyone that I was tired and didn't want to talk about anything until the next day.

Well, the next day was Sunday... and guess who was starting a revival.

You guessed it!

An angry, cynical, engaged man who couldn't even stand himself.

Carry went with me to church the next day. We didn't say anything to each other. It was so hard, because as soon as we walked into the church everyone was "congratulating" us on our upcoming nuptials, and I still wasn't so sure that I wanted to be a part of them.

You see, something had flipped.

At the beginning of our engagement, I was excited; Carry was nervous. Now Carry was excited, and I had cold feet.

When I first mentioned having cold feet, Carry said, "You better buy some socks."

The sermons from that week's revival are posted on YouTube at the time of this writing. I can watch them and almost become sick to my stomach.

I put on a good show. That's not to say that God didn't anoint me and give me grace to preach His Word, but when I look at that preacher with his suit and tie on, I know what was going on in his heart. He was battling. He was wrestling.

The ministry that I loved so much had become a dread. I preached to people night after night about the hope that we have in Christ, but would go home and try to drown my sorrows with temporary substances. I was miserable, but I couldn't reach out to anyone for help. Everybody came to me for help! I was a preacher.

I'm afraid too many times Christians (and especially preachers) fight private battles and feel like they are all alone. Preacher, or Christian, you are not alone. If you are hurting, don't carry that hurt by yourself. Find a Christian brother or sister whom you can confide in. Don't be afraid of their judgment or condemnation. God doesn't expect you to carry that burden alone.

It was the last week of October, and I was out of town preaching a revival. Carry would call every day to check on me, and I would roll my eyes when her number would come up on my phone.

I was losing a good thing, and I didn't realize it until it was almost too late.

CHAPTER 10

November 1, 2015. It was a Sunday morning. It was Homecoming at my dad's church. I had been out of town all week. Carry and I had spent a few hours together on Saturday afternoon, but my mind was still unsettled.

She was sitting in the front row. I was sitting at the keyboard. Tensions were high. Our wedding was six days away, and I was still planning on bailing. She just didn't know it yet.

After church, there was a spread that would've fed the children of Israel in the wilderness. I remember sitting at a round table with Carry, Jacob, Mom and Dad. People constantly stopped by to "congratulate" us. Carry says she can remember my whole countenance dropping when people would stop by and talk about the wedding.

She left early and went home to our house on Kerr Street. I hung out with Jacob at Mom and Dad's.

But it was time to sit down and have a serious conversation.

Money had been spent. Dresses and tuxes had been ordered. A venue had been reserved. Invitations had been sent out. Was there going to be a groom?

When Carry and I sat down together on November 5 (two days before our wedding) she asked me point-blank, "Are we getting married?" She said, "Tyler, I don't need an unsure answer from you. I need to know how you are feeling and what you are thinking." I was seated at my keyboard at home and I was picking out melodies and tunes while she was talking.

My only answer was, "I don't know. I don't know."

She finally looked at me and said, "I'm going to be at New Life Church tomorrow night for our rehearsal. I'll see you there."

As she got up to leave, I said, "No need to wait for me. I won't be there."

She stopped, turned around with huge tears in her eyes and said, "You really don't love me, do you?"

My calloused heart wasn't moved. I said, "I care about you, but I don't want to marry you."

She left crying, and I stayed behind my keyboard.

It was late in the evening. She was supposed to be on her way to Lumberton to get together with her bridesmaids and celebrate.

It breaks my heart to imagine such a sweet-hearted girl driving her little black car down those roads from Clinton to Lumberton with tears streaming down her face... because of my calloused heart.

Well, I don't know what happened, but as I sat in my room and looked up at the tuxedo I was supposed to wear, every memory of our time together flashed before my eyes. All of a sudden, the calloused shell that had encased my heart for months broke in an instant and I called my mom (who was at New Life Church setting up for the wedding rehearsal but was about to tear it all down because of my decision to cancel the wedding), but there was no answer.

Texts were going out that the wedding was canceled, and I was frantic to get a hold of somebody before it was too late!

I called Carry. No answer. I called my mom's friend who was helping her. No answer.

Finally, my mom called. I said, "Don't tear anything down! The wedding is on!" She said, "I just talked to Carry. The wedding is not on." I said, "It is now," and hung up.

I called Carry... over and over and over. She finally answered, and I said, "Look, the wedding is on. Please come back to Mom and Dad's. I need to talk to you."

At almost 11 p.m., we sat on my mom and dad's couch and I apologized to her. When she walked through the door that night, I felt in my heart like I did the night I first saw her at my revival and said, "Goodness gracious."

All I know is that God must have softened my heart in that moment, but I almost lost my wife.

The very next night, I walked into New Life Church in Lumberton, North Carolina, for our wedding rehearsal.

Talk about awkward!

Here were my wife's people who knew how I had treated her. Here were people who usually would've talked to me, but everybody was silent. The only people talking to me were my clan.

But as the wedding rehearsal rolled on, the mood lightened.

As I left that night after a bunch of cake, sparklers, and floating lanterns, I knew I would be returning to marry a remarkable woman.

I spent the rest of the night and the next morning with my cousin Chandler and my brother Jacob. We laughed so hard my stomach hurt. It was the first time I had felt true joy in a long time.

November 7, 2015. It was time to head back to Lumberton. This time, I was decked out in a tux. I arrived at the church a few hours early.

As the wedding ceremony got closer and closer, people were coming in and I was greeting them as they came in.

Nobody told me the groom wasn't supposed to be socializing!

Then it was time.

I had made fun of my dad who, the night before his wedding, cried during his rehearsal. I talked so much junk to the people who were crying at our rehearsal. But let me tell you something...

After the wedding party marched in, after those back doors closed for a few minutes and opened again and my wife, decked out in a beautiful white dress walked out holding on to her daddy, I ugly-cried.

Anyone who attended our wedding will tell you that the only word to describe the atmosphere was "grace." It was a graceful ceremony. There was a sweet Spirit of the Lord present. I felt like I had been born again all over again!

When that beautiful bride walked down the aisle and smiled at me (actually, she laughed because I was crying), my knees buckled.

That's when it sunk in, "That's my wife."

The ceremony was beautiful. It was much like a church service.

Our reception was small, but it was nice. It was small because the venue had been canceled. (I'm not sure why. We won't point any fingers at this point.)

After a nice time with family and friends, we jumped into Carry's little black car and made the drive from Lumberton to Morehead City, North Carolina, in a torrential downpour.

It was a Saturday night. We were on our way to a condominium to stay the night, because guess who had to preach a Homecoming service the next day...

Now, I did ask Carry if she wanted me to cancel it, but she said, "No. I want to enter our marriage doing what we are going to be doing," so while this was the start of our honeymoon, it was also a ministry venture. I was preaching at one church on Sunday morning and another on Sunday night. Then we would wake up early Monday morning to go to Disney World for a week!

We settled into our condominium some time after midnight.

The next day, we spent preaching.

Monday morning, my wife and I (I still called her my fiancée for the longest time) headed to Disney World.

When we came home a week later, my parents had worked on our Kerr Street house. Because of my bad behavior and poor choices before our wedding, I couldn't stand to drive onto the property, much less walk into the house. Every time I saw the blinds, I thought about Dad. Every time I walked into the den, I thought of how I had treated Carry. I couldn't stand the house that had started out as a blessing.

But when we walked through the front door that night, it felt like home. It was so cozy.

The day of our wedding rehearsal, I had knelt on the floor in my home office and repented. I asked God to forgive me for the choices I had made, the attitudes I had portrayed, and I asked Him to place His hand upon my life afresh before I became a husband. I knew I couldn't adequately love anyone until my love for Christ was back in order. I feel like this prayer set the tone for our Kerr Street house to feel so much like home.

We hadn't been married a week, but our journey was about to take an unexpected turn.

CHAPTER 11

Do you remember that prayer I told you I blurted out one day: "Lord, give me a pastor's heart"? He answered it.

Don't pray something if you don't mean it!

Although I enjoyed evangelism, I noticed my heart wasn't in it anymore. I was also having a lot of challenges with my voice holding out. I was to the point where I couldn't even get past the third night of a four-night revival before my voice was completely gone.

I talked to my conference headquarters at the time and asked for a meeting with the regional director. I expressed my desire to start pastoring, and he kindly met with me.

I filled in at a few churches here and there, but within a few weeks the General Superintendent called me and said, "Tyler, a church has just come available. It's the perfect church for you. You have a meeting tomorrow with the Regional Director in Clinton."

Guess where we met--Bojangles in Clinton. A special place for me, I guess.

The Regional Director told me all about the church. He put me on schedule to preach there, and I was so excited.

Carry was as supportive as I could have ever asked. We kept preaching revivals here and there, but finally the Sunday came for us to try out at this new church.

We made the 45-minute drive and mingled in the crowd before the service started. I preached, and the congregation really seemed receptive to the message.

On the way home, Carry and I talked about everything we could think of about the church: the pros, the cons, the possibilities, the impossibilities.

For several weeks, I preached at this church. I preached on Wednesday nights, Sunday nights, Sunday mornings, and even attended the New Years Eve service that year.

When it became apparent that our names were going to be run for the pastorate position, we started doing some serious praying.

My parents weren't too thrilled about me leaving the home church. Other supporters of our ministry told me that I didn't need to try to pastor a church. But Carry and I felt at home at this church. And nobody knew about my "Lord, give me a pastor's heart" prayer.

When we would go to preach revivals, oftentimes Carry would lean over and say, "I miss 'our' church."

On February 3, 2016, I received a 96% vote to become the pastor of this historical church in Wallace, North Carolina.

This church had a parsonage located about a mile and a half from the church itself. Although Carry was still working in Clinton, we moved to the parsonage.

I know I have repeatedly recounted instances of being sick in this book, but in March I became really nauseated one weekend. It was right before church one Sunday morning, so I took a pill to ease the nausea and felt fine. It started to become a weekly thing. I was living off nausea pills and starting to feel like I lived in outer space.

After an endoscopy, the gastroenterologist determined that it was acid reflux that was making me sick. I started taking medicine for that, and I seemed to be better.

In May, I started getting sick again. It only happened on Sunday mornings. I would be fine Monday-Saturday, but Sundays I would be miserably sick.

One week, it hit me on a Thursday. I was the guest speaker

in the high school and middle school chapel services at Harrells Academy in Harrells, North Carolina. I was fine during the high school chapel, but just before the middle school chapel, this sickness hit me. Jacob and Adam (a family friend of ours) were with me. I preached through the nausea, and as soon as the chapel service was over, we headed to New Hanover Hospital in Wilmington. After spending several hours there, it was determined that nothing was wrong with me.

You don't know how frustrated I was to keep hearing that, when I knew something was wrong with me!

My mom suggested that my wife take a pregnancy test. She did, but she wasn't pregnant. I felt like I was, though!

Finally, I went to my primary care doctor... the same man who had diagnosed me with Type I Diabetes when I was 7 years old.

After asking some questions, he leaned back on his stool and said, "Tyler, you're suffering from depression."

Who knew that nausea was a symptom of depression?

He said, "You've been sitting here for about ten minutes. Look at how you're sitting. You're on the edge of the exam table, your hands are in a constant wringing motion. You look as if you're waiting for someone to pounce on you. Your nerves are in a bind."

He prescribed me some medicine for depression.

After a few days, I felt a whole lot better!

The sickness stopped. I felt calmer. Of course, I had people telling me to "throw the pills away and trust God," but I happen to believe that God answers our prayers through doctors and medication. Some people have told me, "Depression isn't real," but it is very real and can be treated, just like cancer can be treated.

You see, this sickness would hit me at around 10 or 10:30

on Sunday mornings. Service started at 11 a.m. There were many Sundays I would race to my car, head home, and lie on the bathroom floor or on the couch until I could get relief. Many times I would walk out onto the stage behind the choir, preach, shake a few hands, and rush home.

There were 78 in regular attendance when we arrived at this church. By the summer of 2016, we were running in the 120s on Sunday mornings. We had started a radio program, and the services were enriched with the presence of the Lord.

It was amazing to witness not only numerical growth, but spiritual growth as well.

When I was an evangelist, I could get a church jumping and jiving by saying, "It's time to get out of the book of Numbers and get back into the book of Acts!"

I have preached all my life that numbers are not a measure of success, and I still agree to an extent. However, every number represents a soul. You may hear me talk about numbers throughout this book. I'm not bragging on myself or gauging success by it, but you must admit that the more people you have on board, the more ears are hearing the Gospel.

That doesn't mean they're listening, but they're hearing, and that's a step.

With the sickness diagnosed and behind me, I started focusing on the fall months of 2016.

Guess who I booked for our Homecoming service--Rev. David Smith. The man I wanted to be like so much in my evangelistic years. It felt so unreal, introducing this man to a congregation I was pastoring.

Attendance continued to increase, and I was excited about the momentum we were feeling.

In February, I was praying one Saturday night and out of nowhere, I felt like the Lord was impressing upon me to fast. I didn't know what I was fasting for, but I told my wife I was going to start a 40-day fast that would culminate on April 30.

When God tells you to do something, don't ask questions. Just do it!

This was my first pastorate. New people were coming in every week. Some stepped up, ready to take volunteer positions. With no pastoral experience whatsoever, I handled situations with immaturity. I didn't know how to handle such rapid growth. I upset some people. I overstepped some bounds. I made a lot of mistakes. I didn't take the advice of those older and wiser than me. And amid the growth, I blew it.

No, I wasn't unfaithful to my wife, although to an extent, I feel like I was.

I've heard it said that the first year of marriage is the hardest. We are testimonies of that!

Not only were we a young newlywed couple, we were pastoring our first church. Do you know how many times we ended up at each other's throats? I hope the parsonage didn't have any built-in cameras, because if it did, they've got some stories to tell.

Do you know that Carry contemplated leaving me?

"That's normal." No, I was making a huge mistake. I was putting church before my marriage. "Well, bless God, that's the sacrifice of ministry." No, that's the stupidity of a deceived mind. While I love ministry and the church, no ministry is worth your family; if you are a failure at home, you are not a success anywhere else.

I was reaching all of these people, but I was starting to lose my marriage because I was pushing Carry to the back burner.

Side note: show your pastor's wife some love. I know we have appreciation days for pastors, and that is all well and good, but the wives oftentimes stand in the background. Churches don't realize how integral a pastor's wife is.

I wasn't physically unfaithful to my wife. I didn't misuse any of the church's finances. I simply didn't know how to handle growth and change, and after a church meeting (called by me) I turned in my resignation on April 23, 2017 (my 24th birthday).

There was right and wrong on both sides. I'm not here to point fingers at anyone, or say that I regret taking the pastoral position of that church. I don't, because I learned so many valuable lessons that I probably wouldn't have learned in a classroom. Hands-on experience is something special!

But I will never forget that afternoon. My phone rang from the time the meeting was over until the time I finally just powered it off late that night.

There were a lot of people who were hurting and confused, but I made up my mind that I had received enough calls for one day.

So Carry and I held each other tight that night with our Chorkie Jazzy and our chihuahua Leo at our feet, with the Lord Jesus Christ above our heads watching every move… never slumbering or sleeping.

Chapter 12

Amid the calls of support, the calls of rage, and the moving boxes scattered through the parsonage, I received calls to preach revivals. I was grateful! I was out of a job. Carry and I were grateful for opportunities that were quickly opening.

But I had a group of people who were still calling me "Pastor."

A friend of mine called me a few days after the church meeting and said, "If we have service in my backyard, will you preach?" At first I said "No," because I didn't want any conflict with our previous church. I realized we were dealing with a classic "church split," but I didn't want to cause any more harm.

However, I finally obliged that I would gladly attend, encourage and pray, but I didn't want it to be a "service."

On April 30 the last day of that 40-day fast I didn't fully understand, 37 people gathered in my friends' backyard (in PinHook, incidentally--remember, that's where I held my first revival after the big Bethel revival) and the presence of the Lord was there.

At the close of our time together, I said, "I don't know what we are going to do from here, but come back Thursday night and we'll meet again."

What was I doing?

That Thursday night, about 13 people came back and we had a round-room discussion on what a church really is. After our discussion and prayer, we talked about our future.

It was decided that we would start having Sunday morning services at Mill Swamp Community Building, and small group meetings on Thursday nights at my friends' house where we'd had our first get-together.

The next Sunday, about 60 people gathered at Mill Swamp Community Building. I was blown away. Some were just visiting. Some were just checking out this new work. Others were planning on sticking around for the long haul.

We knew we couldn't rent the community building forever. Although I didn't even know where Carry and I were going to live, I knew we were going to have to eventually find a building.

We decided, however, that before we found a building, we probably needed a name.

As we all called out suggestions, I think we ended up with 30-some names on a sheet of paper. Some of them were rather humorous. My initial idea was "The Encounter," but after several people said that sounded too spooky and like a nightclub, I gave that one up.

Finally, someone spoke up and said, "What about Imprint?"

You see, in the final sermon I had preached at our previous church, I talked about the difference between being buried and being planted. If something is buried, you're done with it. But if something is planted (like a seed), the planting serves a purpose. It is dark and damp (just like something being buried), but new life will ultimately spring up.

A synonym for "plant" is "imprint," and our key verse was II Corinthians 3:2-3, "Your very lives are a letter that anyone can read by just looking at you. Christ himself wrote it - not with ink, but with God's living Spirit; not chiseled into stone, but carved into human lives - and we publish it." (The Message).

Not only were we believing for "new life" through this

season of planting, but we wanted to make an "imprint" on our community. We wanted our church to be a place of trust, a safe haven for those who were hurting and lost.

That night, a unanimous decision was made: our church would be called The Imprint Church.

Within two days, we were out looking for a building.

We found one in Beulaville, but it seemed like every time we tried to move forward with it, something stood in our way.

One of the ladies in our congregation pulled me to the side one day and said, "Pastor, I don't have peace about this building. If this is where you feel we need to be, my family and I will gladly serve here, but I just don't have peace."

There was a church in Duplin County known as River of Life. It was just off Highway 41, within a mile or so of the city limits of Chinquapin. (Remember that city?)

It wasn't even a mile from where Highway 50 and Highway 41 run together. Not even a mile from where I had sat a few years before and felt "stuck." Another "Bethel moment" in the books.

But as people asked me to find out about the price and the availability of the building, I shot the idea down. I told them, "There may not be very many people that attend there, but they still use that building."

Many people insisted that the building was empty, but I said, "No. There's a church there." One day, my wife and I drove by the old River of Life and I pulled into the parking lot. The grass was high and unmaintained. When I walked to the front door, I noticed the doors were chained up with huge chains.

I was about to have to admit something I didn't want to admit: I was wrong! Nobody had used this building in a while.

But my saving grace was that I didn't know whom to get

in contact with.

It appeared that the building was, indeed, vacant, but there was no "For Sale" sign in the yard. There was no number on the door. The only thing I knew to do was to call the North Carolina Assemblies of God District Offices. My wife took it upon herself to make that phone call. She got in contact with someone, told them our situation, and was told she would be called back within a day.

Carry and I went our separate ways as she went to work and I went to do the things I had to do that day.

On the way back home through Chinquapin, I stopped at the old River of Life. I pulled my barely-running S-10 pickup truck to the back of the property. I got out and sat Indian-style in the grass. I could take you to that exact spot. It's another "Bethel." I looked up at the building and I said something along the lines of, "God, this is impossible. I know you can do anything, but this is impossible." Talk about talking out of both sides of my mouth. I said, "God, I love these people who have helped establish The Imprint. They've been through a lot, and Lord, I don't want to get their hopes up. So please let us down gently. And if there is any way this is your will, make it plain."

I don't know how many times I cupped my hands over my eyes and leaned against the windows. I guess I thought I was going to see something different each time.

After a while, a friend of mine stopped by and we decided to go to Buck's Corner.

If you are from Duplin County, you know that Buck's Corner is the only thing in Chinquapin. For those of you who don't know, it's a gas station, but they can serve up some tasty hot dogs. So he and I drove right up the road to Buck's Corner. I had a hopeful heart to hear back from the Assemblies of God before the day ended.

I was inside looking for a snack when my friend came in and said, "Do you want to see the inside of the church?" I was thinking, "Oh, no. He's gotten a wild idea and he has thought of a clever way to break in." I said, "Of course I want to see the inside of the church, but we can't break in. God won't honor that." He said, "No. The guy who has the keys is out here beside your truck." I said, "Don't play with me like that," because I was kind of bummed that we couldn't get in.

He said, "God as my witness, he is out there."

I quickly paid for my food (I know it would be more dramatic to say I dropped it and ran out, but I was hungry). When I went out to the truck, Pastor Gary Manning was sitting there.

I knew Pastor Gary because he went to Bible College with my dad, and we had previously preached a funeral together. We spoke briefly, and he said, "Do you want to see inside River of Life?" I said, "Sure!"

"Follow me," he said, and a Ford followed by an S-10 followed by another Ford pulled back out onto Hwy 41, headed to the old River of Life.

When we arrived, Pastor Gary said, "You didn't see me, but as you pulled out, I was pulling into the driveway. I wasn't sure if I needed to follow you, but I felt prompted to. Let me take these chains off the door," and he let us in a side door that led to the back hallway of the church.

When we walked in, there was no carpet on the ground because back in October 2016 during Hurricane Matthew, River of Life was flooded.

I cannot express the ideas that were flying through my mind as we walked through the flooded building. I was thinking of the previous congregation and the work they had done for God while in this building. I thought about the people who were now known as The Imprint. I was still in shock that we were IN the building!

After a long conversation, Pastor Gary looked at me and said, "Do you have an offer?"

I said, "Pastor Gary, I am in love with this building, but there is no way we can afford it." He pulled out a piece of paper and said, "Write down an offer anyway."

I snuck away from Pastor Gary and called my wife. I could hardly contain my excitement. I told her the offer I felt like writing down, she agreed, and we made our first "pastoral decision" over the phone.

When I handed him the paper, he looked at it, folded it, put it in his pocket, and said, "I'll get back with you."

He was showing the building to a few men the next day who wanted to turn it into a storage building.

The next afternoon, he called me and said that the District wanted a meeting with me the following Tuesday.

This was on Wednesday. I asked him if he would let us in on Thursday night for some of our congregation to see it. He obliged, and that Thursday a handful of us toured the old River of Life and started praying as we walked through the building. We prayed for God's will.

I was standing in the sanctuary praying and saw people passing by the windows. When I walked outside, I saw that several of our congregants had ended up walking the property and praying. I know people who were passing by on Highway 41 thought we were insane. Nevertheless, we prayed for God's will to be done.

When I left that night, I had such a peace in my heart.

CHAPTER 13

The following Tuesday I had a meeting in Selma, North Carolina, at the District Offices of the Assemblies of God.

I walked in late. A wreck on I-95 had traffic backed up for miles. Thankfully, some of the employees of the District Offices had been caught in the traffic as well, so the men I was meeting with were aware of the delay.

I sat at a round table with Dr. Rick Ross and Dr. Randall Rogers. I was nervous, but I told them our situation and expressed our interest in the building they owned in Chinquapin.

Dr. Rogers explained to me that the property had recently been appraised for $550,000. My offer had been $250,000.

I was $300,000 below what the property was appraised for.

However, they quickly let me know that my offer had been accepted.

We signed a lease agreement that day and discussed the other legalities that had to be taken care of.

When I jumped back into my truck, my excitement was through the roof. I don't know if I was more excited or relieved. I called everyone I could think of to let them know that the days of renting the community building were over and that God had answered our prayers.

Two nights later, on a Thursday night, we held our first service in our new building. There was no carpet, and there were several repairs that needed to be made. But this was home... and that was exactly what it felt like.

That Saturday, we all pitched in and hauled off trash,

made "yard sale" piles, rearranged the stage and the setup of the sanctuary, and had a wonderful time tidying up our new home.

Before we knew it, it was Sunday morning, May 28, 2017. We had organized on April 30. Less than a month later we were in a building that granted, we were leasing, but we were in a "rent-to-own" contract. This was ours, by the grace of God.

And let me tell you, it was ONLY by the grace of God. I didn't have $5 in my pocket when I made that offer, much less $250,000! It was a step of faith that God honored.

God never lets us see the whole picture.

If He had told me why He was calling me to a 40-day fast, I would've probably run the other direction. It wouldn't have even made sense at that time.

Small steps of faith lead to large acts of God. You've come along too late to tell me it isn't true.

On May 28, 70-some people gathered at The Imprint.

At first, we weren't sure if we would ever worship together again. We were all blindsided and devastated.

Then, we worshiped in a backyard.

Then, we worshiped in a living room.

Then, we worshiped in a community building.

Now, we had a home. God had been faithful.

One thing I can say about that small congregation: they stuck together. They prayed. They worshiped. They loved their God. They loved their church family. And they worked... hard. Despite the negative comments floating around the community, and the way many of them were treated because of their association with this new church plant, these people kept their eyes on the prize, and I was privileged to lead them.

We were experiencing rapid growth. By mid-July, our attendance was consistently at 100.

As news spread that our church was not running traditionally, we got labeled as a cult.

For example, we don't have "members" at Imprint. We have "owners," because "members" of organizations have rights. If you sign up to become a "member" of an organization, there are rights that belong to you. However, "owners" have responsibilities. I've caught a little bit of flack for that, too.

Let me pause right here and say if you can't take criticism, you will give up in leadership before you ever get started. You can't please everybody. People are going to question your motives and make you question yourself. Ministry is not as glamorous as some people seem to think. As a matter of fact, preaching is just the fun part!

Season your decisions with prayer, follow the leading of the Lord, and when you know that you're doing what you're doing at the command of the Lord, criticism will roll off of you like water off of a duck's back. Trust me.

It hurt my feelings then, but it's more of a joke now… at one point, I was compared to Jim Jones. Now, we often tell each other not to "drink the Kool-Aid."

One late afternoon, I was getting ready for a revival service when Carry came home from work. She came into the bedroom of our rental home with her hands behind her back. She looked… mischievous. I couldn't quite read her. I said, "What's going on?" She said, "I have something to tell you. Please don't be mad." I thought, "Oh, boy. The car has been wrecked. Or she's gotten a ticket and knows we can't afford it. She's made a bad decision." Poor Carry. I didn't think anything positive.

She sat on the edge of the bed and pulled a pregnancy

test from behind her back. I looked down and saw that it was positive.

The air caught in my throat. I couldn't speak! I said, "Are you telling me that I'm going to be a daddy?" With tears in her eyes she said, "Yes, I'm pregnant."

I wanted to tell somebody, but she didn't want the news to get out until we had been to the OB/GYN doctor to get an official report.

I'm pretty sure that I sprouted wings and flew to church that night. My heart was overwhelmed. Not only was our church flourishing, but now our family was growing.

We had planned on waiting several years before trying for a baby, but God had other plans, and we couldn't have been more excited.

After the confirmation from the OB/GYN doctor, we waited to announce our pregnancy to our church on our first-annual "Offering Fit for a King" Sunday. (It's where owners bring their tithes and best offerings.)

Our offering that morning was two little moccasin shoes!

At the time of this writing, my wife is very pregnant, and our baby girl is scheduled to arrive in April 2018.

God is adding a travel partner on this "journey," and I already know that she's a daddy's girl!

CHAPTER 14

In September we accepted 65 owners into our church. I dedicated a few babies, and we had a baptismal service where we baptized at least 13 people. It was a remarkable day in our history.

Carry and I had been paying on a Disney vacation for almost a year. After church one Sunday late September, we headed for the Sunshine State. We didn't come back home until the next Sunday night. I had felt like it was time to take a break from everything. The church had been planted, the ball was rolling, and now it was time to relax.

But planting a church is like having a baby. Most parents don't leave their newborns with just anybody. It's a while before mom is ready to leave that baby, and before baby is okay with that. Our volunteers kept the church running like a Swiss watch while we were gone, but we didn't have it as "made" as we had thought we had it.

Many of our volunteers had come from our previous church. Because of our rapid growth, many of them did not have time to grieve, forgive, or heal. Bitterness had started springing up.

The relaxed, loving atmosphere of Imprint had turned into a snappy, strained atmosphere.

On Sunday mornings we were ranging 120-140, but there was a storm brewing behind the scenes. Tensions were rising. Unspoken frustrations were getting ready to explode.

In October, we closed on the loan for our building. Our original offer was for $250,000. At some point in the process, the loan closing was lowered to $185,000. On October 26, we closed on the loan for $150,000.

I still love telling that part of the story.

However, by December our volunteers at church had handled all the pressure they could, and one Sunday night I watched Imprint slowly unravel… or so I thought.

When I left our property that night, I said to Carry, "I'm afraid this church is falling before it even gets a chance to stand."

I called a meeting with our volunteers on Tuesday of that week. Leading up to that meeting, I spent time with men of God such as my dad, Pastor Gary (the man who showed us the building), Pastor Darian (my high school teacher), and Pastor Larry Parker (one of those preachers I have boxes of tapes of). They poured invaluable wisdom into me.

You know, the best leaders are lifelong learners. If we stop learning, we stop leading. It's just that simple.

I guess I'm saying all this for one reason: don't ever stop learning from the older generation that has blazed this path before us.

That Tuesday night the volunteers and I prayed together, cried together, and laughed together. What I had thought was an unraveling was actually a rebuilding.

I can't explain it, but after that Tuesday night meeting the tension was relieved, and the atmosphere of love and grace started resurfacing. I'm not saying that everybody immediately got over their hurt, but a process of restoration began.

Planting a church is a unique venture. A lot of times when a minister accepts a traditional church that has been in existence for several years, he is going into a pre-formed atmosphere. Planting a church is different in that the founders set the tone for the atmosphere.

I have always wanted Imprint to be a church where

"strangers" feel at home. So far, that has been the factor that is commented upon the most: the atmosphere of our church.

I didn't want to lose that over trivial matters.

I've also learned that a true leader does not point fingers at those he leads. If there is a flaw in leadership at Imprint, the buck stops here.

I wish I had trained my volunteers before launching them into ministries with others who were also inexperienced.

That's not to say that our volunteers haven't done a wonderful job, but I believe their responsibilities would have been a lot easier had I offered to help them.

At the time of this writing, all of that is behind us. We've hit some rough patches, but the journey of life is full of them.

The Imprint Church is not a perfect church by any means. I heard a preacher say one time that if you find a perfect church, don't join it because you'll mess it up.

We don't claim to be the only church that's right. As a matter of fact, I have established wonderful friendships with other pastors in our community. God has allowed us the opportunity to open a college program that I have the privilege of teaching every Tuesday night.

I preach on Sunday mornings and teach on Tuesday nights and Thursday nights. There is no higher privilege than preaching and teaching the Word of God.

I feel like the most blessed pastor in the world to pastor The Imprint, and I get to do it all with my precious wife by my side. God has brought us a long way for us to not even be a year old yet.

It's been a journey so far, but I can hardly wait to see what's going to happen next. I can't help but feel... that it's just getting started.

CHAPTER 15

So that's my story. My life has been a true journey so far, but right now I'm as content as I've ever been. I'm married to the love of my life. Our baby is on the way. I pastor a church that God has blessed us to be able to start from the ground up. I get to teach Bible College and develop men and women for ministry. I do all of this while living close to my family (we are still very close-bonded).

But sometimes our testimony doesn't encourage people. It discourages them. Maybe you're in a "stuck" position right now. Can I tell you... that God doesn't love me any more than He loves you? I know what it's like to see other people succeed and wonder when it's going to happen for me.

Like I said, my life isn't perfect. Nobody's is. But I have come a long way... and you will too.

The accounts recorded in this book didn't happen overnight. I have no way of describing the long "in-between" periods. But the Bible promises in Philippians 2:13 that if God starts a work in you, He is faithful to complete it.

I have a couple of closing comments I want to leave with you.

In life, there are kissers and cleavers. In the Old Testament, there was a man named Elimelech. Elimelech was married to Naomi, and together they had two sons: Mahlon and Chilihon. Elimelech took his family away from their hometown of Bethlehem-Judah and led them to Moab. While in Moab, Elimelech died... along with Mahlon and Chilihon. Before Mahlon and Chilihon died, they married two young ladies: Ruth and Orpah.

When Naomi decided to go back to her hometown, she told her two daughters-in-law to go back to their hometowns. The Bible says Orpah kissed Naomi on the cheek and headed back home, but Ruth "clave unto" her. It is here that Ruth made the famous statement, "Where you go, I'll go. Where you stay, I'll stay. Your people will be my people. Your God will be my God." (Ruth 1:16 NIRV).

Kissers and cleavers. Kissers will hang out with you as long as it's convenient for them, and as long as you're walking the path they're walking. But the moment it becomes convenient for them to depart from your life, they will plant a wet kiss on your cheek and move on. Cleavers, however, say, "You're stuck with me."

Throughout my ministry, I've had kissers. But I've had plenty of cleavers, too. Don't mix the two up, and don't let the kissers discourage you from cherishing the cleavers.

I feel like God has dealt with me in stages and will continue to deal with me that way. He has only promoted me to another level when I have passed the one I'm currently on.

When I was a teenager preaching in small, pastor-less churches, God was allowing me the opportunity to develop my speaking skills and my sermon-building skills. That's not to say that those places and that season were any less important in my life, but God puts us in obscure seasons for a reason. Don't try to stand in the spotlight if God has put you on the back side of the wilderness. He has a reason for doing that!

Also, don't chase titles or positions. A lot of people get caught up in being called by a title. Don't let a title or position become more important to you than being obedient and usable in the hands of God.

And always respect others. In an earlier chapter, I talked

about a movement I got involved in that focuses on "outward holiness." I am still invited to speak at churches that have an outward focus. I don't go in and lambaste them. I just preach the Gospel to them. I respect their convictions. I don't share them, but I respect them.

It costs zero dollars to be respectful, but it pays in the end. Maybe someone will be encouraged by reading this. Maybe a young minister can learn from the mistakes I've made. Maybe this real-life story will spark hope in you. Maybe a dream or a passion you've had is lying dormant in the back recesses of your heart. God is literally allowing me to live my dream in His season. He'll do it for you, too.

Don't despise your journey, and remember it won't end until we enter eternity. You may have felt like it was going to end prematurely, but God always finishes what He starts.

And that... is my journey... that's just getting started.

CPSIA information can be obtained
at www.ICGtesting.com
Printed in the USA
FFOW03n1807060618
46996580-49284FF